How Can I Deal With...?

My Parents' Divorce

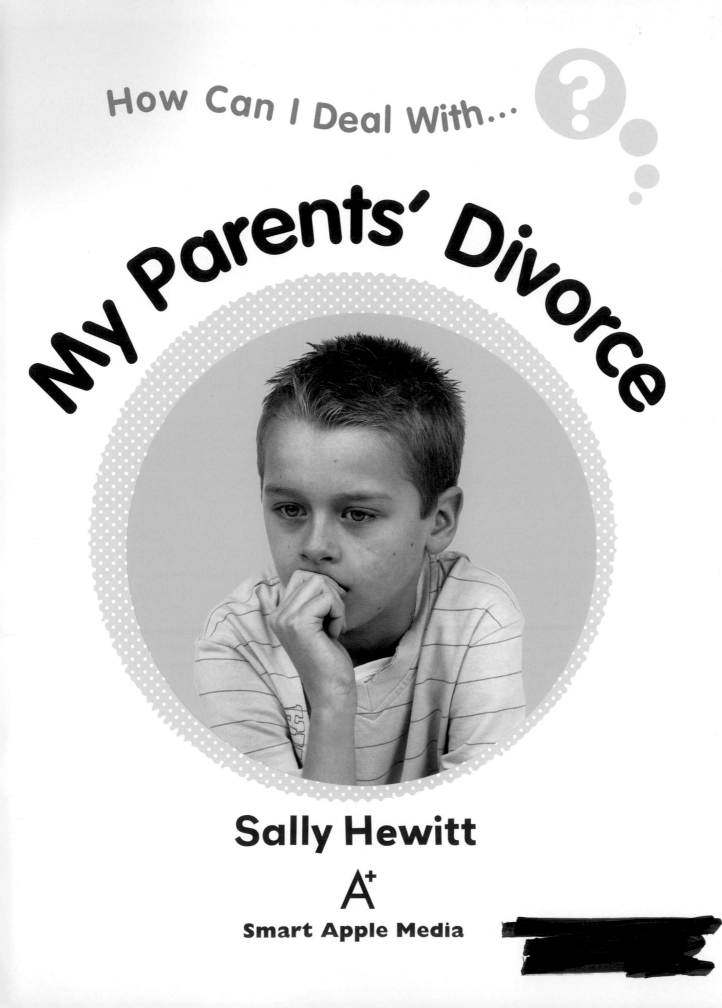

Sally Hewitt

A+

Smart Apple Media

Smart Apple Media is published by
Black Rabbit Books
P.O. Box 3263, Mankato, Minnesota 56002

Printed in the United States

Published by arrangement with the Watts
Publishing Group Ltd, London.

Library of Congress Cataloging-in-
    Publication Data

Hewitt, Sally, 1949–
    My parents' divorce / Sally Hewitt.
    p. cm.—(Smart Apple Media. How can
I deal with—)
    Summary: "Case studies and helpful
advice for kids whose parents are getting
divorced"—Provided by publisher.
    Includes index.
    ISBN 978-1-59920-230-3
    1. Children of divorced parents—
Juvenile literature. 2. Divorced parents—
Juvenile literature. 3. Parent and child—
Juvenile literature. I. Title.
HQ777.5.H48 2009
306.89—dc22
                                    2007035711

Picture credits: Graham Bell/Corbis: 29.
John Birdsall/John Birdsall
Photography: 5, 6, 12, 15 17. Rolf
Brenner/zefa/Corbis: 26. Jacky
Chapman/Photofusion : 23.
Jim Craigmyle/Corbis 27. Paul
Doyle/Photofusion: 25.Images
100/Corbis: 7. Zigy
Kaluzny/Stone/Getty Images: 21.
Keystone/Topfoto: front cover main, 8.
Ute Klaphake/Photofusion : 24.
Andersen Ross/Blend Images/Corbis:
14. Ariel Skelley/Corbis: 22. Lee
Snider/Image Works/Topfoto: 4. Paula
Solloway/Photofusion: 18. Liz
Somerville/Photofusion: 19. Loisjoy
Thurston/Bubbles/Alamy: 13. Bob
Watkins/Photofusion: 20.

Series editor: Sarah Peutrill
Art director: Jonathan Hair
Picture researcher: Diana Morris
Design: Susi Martin
Series advisor: Sharon Lunney

**Please note: Some of the photos
in this book are posed by models.
All characters, situations and
stories are fictitious. Any
resemblance to real persons,
living or dead, is purely
coincidental.**

9 8 7 6 5 4 3 2 1

Contents

My Home Isn't a Happy Place to Be Anymore

Holly's mom and dad argue a lot. They never seem to smile or laugh. Holly's home isn't as happy as it used to be. She doesn't invite friends over anymore.

Luli's Story

Holly's my best friend, but she never asks me to come to her house. She always wants to come home with me. She says she wishes my mom and dad were her mom and dad.

Holly's Story

Mom and Dad keep shouting at each other. Sometimes they just don't talk.

If I want a chat or a story or a hug they say, "Go away, Holly! Not now, Holly! Later, Holly."

They never have time for me.

My friend Luli's mom and dad are always smiling.

When I go over to play they say, "Hello, Holly. Lovely to see you."

They take us swimming and we go to the park.

Luli's mom cooks delicious food. We laugh and have fun.

What Can Holly Do?

She can:

✔ try to talk to her mom and dad when they aren't arguing or busy, and

✔ tell them that she wishes they had more time to spend with her and that she wants them all to have fun together.

What Holly Did

I talked to Mom and Dad. They said they were sorry. They said they made each other unhappy, but they did not want to make me unhappy, too.

Luli came over and Mom took us to the park. We had spaghetti for supper. My favorite!

I think Mom and Dad are going to get a divorce.

It helps to talk to your mom or dad.

A Mom's Story

Before my husband and I got divorced, we were very unhappy. We were too busy arguing to notice that our son Chris was unhappy, too.

So when Chris told us that he wanted to leave home and live with his grandparents, we were shocked!

But we were glad Chris told us how he was feeling. It meant we could help him feel better.

We tried not to argue in front of Chris. We made sure we still had happy times with him.

What Is Divorce?

When a husband and wife decide they don't want to be married anymore, they can get a divorce. They sign papers that make them single again.

After a divorce, children usually live with either their mom or dad and visit the one they are not living with. A judge helps to make sure this is fair. Parents divorce each other, not their children. They will always be their children's mom and dad. Divorce is never the children's fault.

My Parents Are Getting a Divorce

Billy knows his parents are getting a divorce, but he doesn't understand what it means. It makes him feel worried and afraid.

Billy's Story

Mom and Dad are getting a divorce but they didn't tell me much about it. My friend Joe's parents got divorced, but I haven't asked him about it. I'm afraid divorce means something bad will happen.

What Can Billy Do?

He can:

✔ ask his parents to tell him what divorce means,

✔ say he is worried about what will happen, or

✔ talk to his friend Joe.

What Billy Did

I asked Mom and Dad what divorce meant, and they explained it. They said they would make sure I agreed about what happened to me.

I talked to my friend Joe. He told me that things had worked out all right for him. I feel better now about what's going to happen.

Joe's Story

When my mom and dad got divorced, Dad moved out and I stayed with Mom.

I see Dad nearly every Sunday, and we go out together. We talk on the phone or email almost every day.

He's renting an apartment, so I'll be able to stay with him soon. We're going on vacation together this summer.

Mom works, and sometimes Grandma picks me up from school and gives me supper.

Things have changed, but it's OK. It's not as bad as I thought it was going to be. Dad and I still have fun.

I Feel Angry with My Mom and Dad

Gracie's parents are getting a divorce. She feels angry with them for letting it happen. She thinks they should try harder to get along with each other.

Gracie's Story

I feel really angry with Mom and Dad. They are going to get a divorce, and they are ruining everything! When my sister and I argue, they tell us to hug and be friends! Why can't they do the same?

What Can Gracie Do?

She can:
- ✔ tell her parents how she feels about the divorce—that she is angry with them and that they should make up, and
- ✔ listen to what her parents say.

What Gracie Did

I told Mom and Dad they were ruining everything. I said, "Why do you have to get a divorce?"

They said they had tried hard to work things out.

They were sad they were getting a divorce. I don't feel so angry with Mom and Dad anymore.

At least that will make them happy!

Alfie was also angry when his mom and dad split up.

Alfie's Story

Last year my dad left my mom, me, and my little sister and went to live with his girlfriend. I was really angry.

Now my little sister and I are supposed to visit Dad every other weekend. I wouldn't go at first. I was so angry with Dad. He shouldn't have left us!

But Mom said she wanted me and Dad to be friends. Now Dad and I have tennis lessons together. We went to the beach last weekend. We have a nice time, but I still haven't been to his new home. Maybe I will soon.

Is My Parents' Divorce My Fault?

Rosa worries that it's her fault her parents are getting a divorce. She thinks she can stop it happening by always being kind and good.

Mo's Story

Rosa and I used to have lots of fun. Sometimes we were quite naughty and got the giggles.

But she's changed. She never wants to be naughty. She even worries about little things like getting her clothes dirty or making a spelling mistake. I don't know what's the matter with her!

Rosa's Story

I haven't told anyone, but Mom and Dad are splitting up. Dad's going to leave home.

Sometimes I can be really naughty. I'm worried that it's my fault they are splitting up. I want to make things better so Mom and Dad will be happy together again. I make them cards and presents, I tidy my room, and I work hard at school. I don't argue with my younger brother and sister.

I think that if I'm very good, maybe they won't get divorced and Dad will stay with us.

What Can Rosa Do?

She can:

✔ talk to someone she trusts, such as her friend Mo, her grandparents, or her teacher,

✔ remember her parents' divorce is not her fault, or

✔ tell her parents how she feels.

What Rosa Did

I talked to my friend Mo. She said when her mom and dad got a divorce, they told her it wasn't her fault. She said it's not my fault either.

There's nothing I can do to make my mom and dad stay together. I wish there was, but at least I don't have to be good all the time, after all!

What's Going to Happen to Me?

Ed is worried about what is going to happen to him when his parents divorce. He thinks everything will change. He doesn't think any of the changes will be good ones.

Sangita's Story

Ed thinks we won't be friends after his mom and dad are divorced.

He's worried he'll have to move and go to a different school.

But I think we can always be friends, whatever happens.

Ed's Story

I know my mom and dad are splitting up, but I don't know what's going to happen to me.

Where will I live and who will I live with—Mom or Dad?

If we have to move, will my new home be as nice as this one?

Will we have enough money?

Will I have to change schools?

Can I still play on the soccer team?

Will I lose all my friends?

Will I still see Grandma and Grandpa?

I'm worried about everything!

What Can Ed Do?

He can:

✔ talk to his mom and dad about his worries—things might not be as bad as he thinks, or

✔ talk to his friends and make plans to keep in touch—they can talk on the phone, e-mail, and visit each other.

What Ed Did

I asked Mom and Dad what was going to happen. They said we were going to sell our house, but they didn't know where my new home will be.

They said if I did change schools, I would make new friends. They promised to help me keep in touch with my old friends and play soccer. I'll still see Grandma and Grandpa.

Sometimes, parents who are getting a divorce can't agree on what to do about money and their children. When that happens, a mediator can help.

A Mediator's Story

An important part of my job is to listen. I listen to both parents, and I listen to the children. I help them all to listen to each other.

They all say what they want to happen and what they think is fair.

I help them make the best plan they can, even if it isn't perfect.

I'm Ashamed about My Parents' Divorce

Louis feels ashamed. He does not want his friends to find out that his parents are divorced.

Louis's Story

I don't want my friends to know what has happened at home. I pretend Dad is still living with us. I don't ask my friends over to my house in case they find out he's gone. I flew my kite with my friend yesterday. I pretended I was happy, and I didn't tell her what is happening.

I feel ashamed that my family doesn't live together anymore.

Louis's Teacher's Story

Louis should not be ashamed at all. Almost half of all children in the United States have parents who have split up, so he isn't the only one. It has happened to several other children in my class, and no one thinks the worse of them.

He can talk to me about it. He can talk to one of the other children whose parents are divorced.

Keeping a secret can make you feel unhappy. It can really help to talk about what is happening to you.

How Can I Love Both My Mom and Dad?

Now that Suzie lives with her mom and just visits her dad, she worries that she won't be able to love them both the same.

Lily's Story

Suzie lives next door. I play with her after school and on weekends.

She keeps worrying about her dad. She thinks she should keep him company and not be having fun here with me.

Suzie's Story

After Mom and Dad's divorce, Dad went to live in an apartment. My sister and I and the dog and cat live with Mom.

I think Dad is lonely and misses us all. I feel bad when I'm having fun and he is on his own. I think I should be with him to cheer him up and keep him company.

But if I lived with Dad, then Mom and my sister would miss me.

I'd miss them too. I don't know what to do. I want everyone to be happy!

What Can Suzie Do?

She can:

✔ talk to her dad on the phone and tell him her news,

✔ send him emails, letters, and photos that will make him smile, and

✔ ask her dad to do the same for her.

What Suzie Did

Sometimes I call Dad, and sometimes he calls me. He says my pictures and letters cheer him up. He tells me nice things he is doing so I don't worry about him.

When I visit, I sometimes take our dog Buster, and we all go for a walk.

Will We Be Happy Again?

When parents get divorced, it can be upsetting for everyone in the family. But things usually work out for everyone in the end.

Fred's Story

When Mom and Dad split up, everyone was upset. I didn't think I'd ever be happy again!

I thought I wouldn't see Mom after she moved out. I thought Dad wouldn't be any good at looking after us.

But I see Mom lots, and we send emails every day too. Dad isn't such a bad

cook after all! I know Mom will always be my Mom and Dad will always be my dad and they'll always love me, whatever happens.

We Survived Our Parents' Divorce

Mick and Ally's parents' divorce was very upsetting, but now everything is much better.

Mick and Ally's Story

Mick: One day, my sister Ally and I had a big fight. I can't remember why.

Ally: Dad really shouted at us. Then Mom shouted at us. Then Dad and Mom had a fight.

Mick: I said to Ally, "Do you think Mom and Dad are going to split up?"

Ally: I said, "If they do, it's our fault because we're naughty and we keep fighting!"

Mick: But Mom and Dad said, "It's not your fault we're getting a divorce."

Ally: We stopped fighting and being naughty, but it didn't make any difference.

Mick: Mom and Dad got a divorce anyway. We were really worried and unhappy. We didn't want things to change.

Ally: We moved to a smaller house, but we stayed at the same school. Dad moved out, but he didn't go far away.

Mick: We talk to Dad on the phone or email him nearly every day. We have fun when we stay with him.

Ally: Mom and Dad have got new partners now, and they've got children. Now we're part of a really big family!

Mick: Things have worked out OK. It's much better than we thought it would be.

Glossary

Ashamed
When you feel ashamed, you are embarrassed. You don't want anyone to know something about you so you keep it a secret.

Divorce
Divorce is when a husband and wife sign legal papers that mean they are not married any more.

Fault
If something is your fault, it means you have caused something bad to happen.

Feelings
Feelings are the way you feel about what is happening to you. You can feel happy or sad, brave or afraid, bored or excited.

Married
Two people are married when they sign papers that make them husband and wife.

Mediator
A mediator helps people who disagree to find a way to agree and make plans for the future.

Single
Someone who is single isn't married. When parents get divorced, they become single again.

Splitting up
Parents split up when they decide not to live together any more and, if they are married, to get a divorce.

Trust
When you trust someone, you know they will tell you the truth and look after you.

Worry
You worry when you don't know what is going to happen and you think of all the bad things that might happen.

Further Information

For Kids:

http://pbskids.org/itsmylife/family/divorce/

Wondering how to deal with divorce? Get advice, ideas, and answers to your questions about divorce. Read comments from kids who have been through divorce already.

www.kidshealth.org/feeling/home_family/divorce.html

Find out what you can do to help your family, your friends, or yourself when people get divorced.

http://www.divorcestep.com/kids/index.shtml

This site has a special kids' section with articles and books about being a stepchild, why parents divorce, and more.

For Parents:

http://www.newlifeafterdivorce.com/

Articles and tips on parenting, financial issues, health, and relationships, for parents adjusting to life after they get a divorce.

http://www.childrenanddivorce.com/

Information for parents, kids, and professionals compiled by two psychologists with a background in counseling.

http://www.kidshealth.org/parent/emotions/feelings/divorce.html

Tips for divorcing parents to help them understand how kids feel.

For Teachers:

http://www.teachablemoment.org/toolbox/toughtimestoolbox.html

This site offers tips for addressing tough issues in your classroom and for helping kids express their feelings.

Note to parents and teachers: Every effort has been made by the publishers to ensure that these Web sites are suitable for children, that they are of the highest educational value, and that they contain no inappropriate or offensive material. However, because of the nature of the Internet, it is impossible to guarantee that the contents of these sites will not be altered. We strongly advise that Internet access is supervised by a responsible adult.

Index

Notes for Parents, Caregivers, and Teachers

When parents separate or divorce, children will be affected. There are many ways that parents, caregivers, and teachers can help children to deal with their parents' divorce and make it as easy for them as possible.

• Children need to know that their parents' divorce is not their fault.
• It helps to have an adult they trust to listen to them and to take their worries seriously.
• Parents can help by not involving children in arguments or asking them to take sides.
• Keeping up routines and discipline can help children feel safe.

Page 5 Holly's Story
Holly's parents are too busy with their own problems to notice that Holly feels unhappy and left out.
• Reassurance and love can help children get through a difficult time.

Page 9 Billy's Story
Billy doesn't know what divorce means and he is thinking the worst.
• Telling children what is going on will help them understand and not be afraid.

Page 12 Gracie's Story
Gracie is angry with her parents for not making things work.
• Knowing that their parents have tried their best can help children be less angry.

Page 15 Rosa's Story
Rosa thinks her parents' divorce is her fault. She wants to make things better.
• Divorce is never the children's fault. It's not up to them to make it all right and they need to be told this.

Page 18 Ed's Story
Ed is worried and afraid that things will be worse for him after the divorce.
• Involving children in plans and keeping them informed will help them not worry. Things are usually not as bad as they fear.

Page 22 Louis's Story
Louis is embarrassed and ashamed about his dad leaving home.
• Secrets can make children feel unhappy. Talking to an adult they trust will help children know that others are going through the same experience.

Page 24 Suzie's Story
Suzie feels responsible for making her parents happy.
• Children are not responsible for their parents' happiness. Parents can discuss ways of having good times with their children and make sure they happen even when they are arguing themselves.

Page 28 Mick and Ally's Story
Children could role-play the parts in this simple playscript. It's an opportunity to reinforce the point that divorce is never the children's fault. They could also write and perform their own play about divorce.